PERFORMING PUPPETS

Written by Michaela Morgan
Photographed by Robert Pickett • Illustrated by Emma Holt

Collins Educational
An imprint of HarperCollinsPublishers

Contents

Puppets... puppets... puppets — *page* 4

Puppets Through the Ages — 5

Basic Techniques — 7

Glove Puppets — 11

Rod Puppets — 14

String Puppets — 15

Shadow Puppets — 16

Recycled Puppets — 18

Putting on a Performance –

The Pied Piper — 19

The Script — 20

The Pied Piper	21
The Townsfolk	23
The Hamelin Children	24
The Rats	26
The Stage	27
Lights and Sound	28
Acting with Puppets	29
Index	31
Further Reading	32
Places to Visit	32

Puppets... puppets... puppets

Today, puppets appear in comedy shows, on television, in theatres, on beaches, in city centres, on village greens and in films. This book offers an introduction to puppets and puppetry, and provides background information as well as instructions for making rod, glove, shadow and string puppets. Guidelines for putting on a puppet performance are also included.

Puppets such as the Muppets appeal to people of all ages throughout the world

In films puppets often play the parts of fantasy figures or monsters. This is the Sammead from the television series *Five Children and It*.

Puppets Through the Ages

A performance of Odessa and the Magic Goat

Puppetry is a very ancient art. It is believed to have been practised in India four thousand years ago. In China, puppetry has been traced back at least two thousand years and all over the East it remains a highly respected and popular art form. Africa also has a long tradition of making puppets and masks. Puppet figures have been found among the ruins of ancient Greece and Rome. In Europe, puppetry first gained popularity in Italy. The word puppet comes from the Italian *pupa,* meaning doll. By the thirteenth century puppetry had spread throughout the continent of Europe and to Britain. European traditions of puppetry were taken to America by explorers but Native American Indians had their own long tradition of puppet dramas featuring animal and human figures. In modern times American puppeteers in particular have been successful at incorporating puppets into film and television.

Travelling Players

Puppeteers often travel from town to town and from country to country with their puppets and their portable theatres. One reason why puppetry has survived is that performances can take place almost anywhere. In the seventeenth century, during the Civil War in England, the Puritans closed the theatres but the puppeteers were able to carry on. They performed in the streets and open places.

Punch and Judy

Punch and Judy shows started 500 years ago in Italy where Punch is called Pulcinello. Because puppeteers travel, very similar stories and characters are found in different countries. In France, Punch is called Polichinelle; in Austria and Germany he's Kasparl; in Spain he's Don Christoval and in Holland he's called Jan Klaasen or Pickle Herring!

Puppet plays are performed in theatres, in the streets and even on beaches

Puppet Plays

Puppets can be used to teach important lessons or to tell historical or religious stories. Sometimes they are used to tell folk and fairy tales and sometimes they are just for entertainment.

This shadow puppet show featuring Mrs Outside/Inside is shown in schools throughout England. It aims to teach children about their bodies and how they can protect themselves against germs and viruses.

Basic Techniques

Simple Puppets

Puppets can range from the very simple to the very sophisticated. The simplest puppet needs nothing more than your own hands.

Draw a body on card and make finger-shaped holes. Your fingers become the puppet's legs.

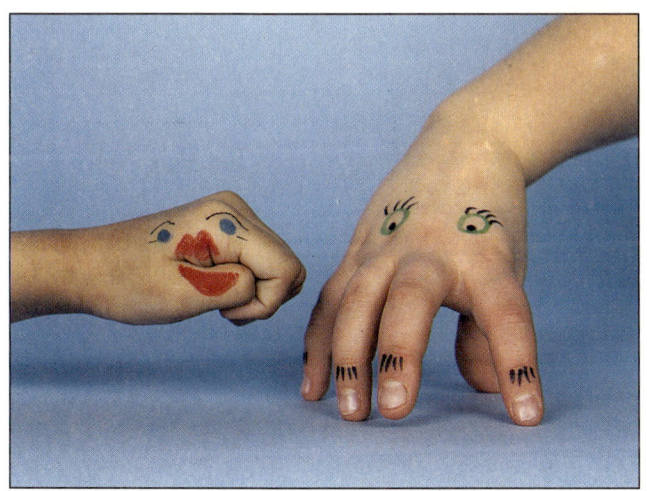

Draw a face on your own hand and practise making different movements with the puppet

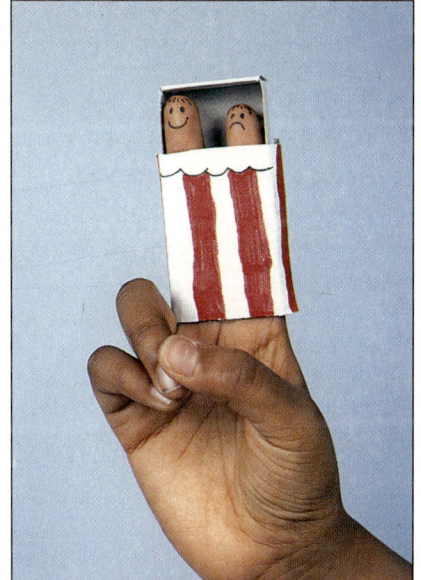

This puppet theatre is a match box. The puppets are fingers with faces drawn on them.

Papier Mâché Heads

Papier mâché is torn up paper, mixed with glue. Many things can be made with it: furniture, props, puppet heads and facial features.

> **You will need:**
> A balloon, PVA-based glue, a bowl, a spoon, old newspapers

2 Tear newspapers into small pieces. Dip the newspaper pieces in the paste.

1 Mix up the glue and water to make a paste. To every one measure of glue, add two measures of water. The paste should look like cream and be able to drop off a spoon.

3 Now you need a base to build on. Blow up a balloon to the size you want the head to be and knot it firmly. This head is suitable for a rod puppet.

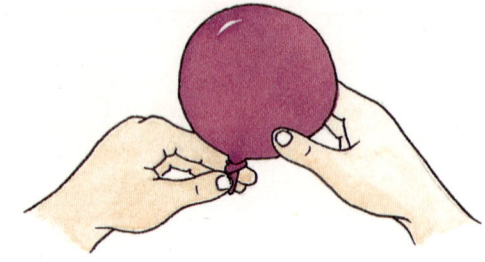

4 For a smaller glove puppet head, crumple up paper into a ball, and use sticky tape to make it into a firm shape.

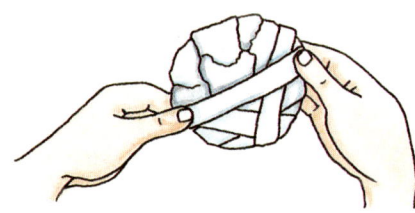

5 Gradually, cover the base with the papier mâché. Don't put too much on at once.

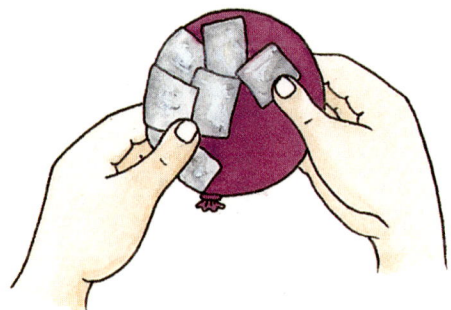

6 Apply two to three layers. Smooth extra paste onto your base if necessary.

7 When the base is fully coated, leave it to dry. This will take at least a day.

Adding Features

Consider the features you want the character to have. If you want the puppet to have a round face and big round cheeks, build up the cheeks with a mixture of tissue paper and glue. Noses can also be built up in the same way. Cover all the tissue paper bulges with a thin layer of papier mâché and leave the head to dry before painting it.

When the heads are painted and dry, add a layer of varnish. This helps to preserve the puppet and gives it a light sheen. Now add features. Go for bold, simple effects on the puppet's face.

1 Make a nose using papier mâché, paint or sticky paper, a piece of an egg box, a bottle cork or a button.

2 Paint, draw or stick on a mouth.

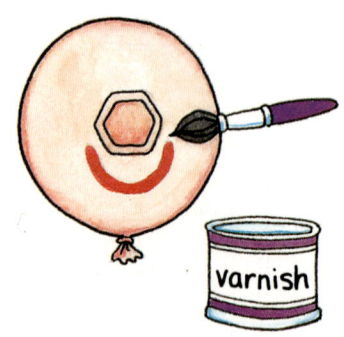

3 Use buttons, ping pong balls, beads or sticky paper to make eyes. Or simply paint them on.

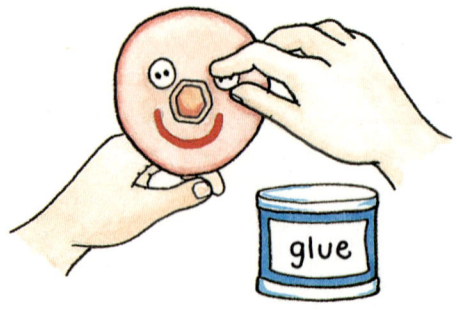

4 Make hair out of wool, straw or cotton wool.

Glove Puppets

Simple Glove Puppets

Glove puppets are worn on the hand and are operated by moving the fingers. Simple glove puppets can be made using old gloves or socks.

Use a black woollen glove to make a spider, or a green washing-up glove to make an octopus. Add eyes and other features.

Make a snake from a long sock. Add eyes and a tongue, and scales to make a dragon.

More Sophisticated Glove Puppets

The Head

You can make a head for a glove puppet from a foam ball or from papier mâché (see pages 8-9).

1 Make a very small hole in the head and try the head on your finger. See page 13 for the different ways of operating a glove puppet. Make the hole the size that fits your finger(s).

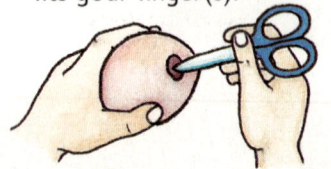

2 Add features to the puppet head.

The Costume

1 Lay two pieces of fabric on top of one another.

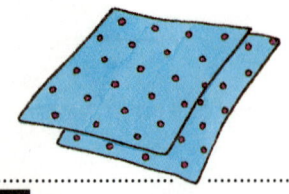

2 Draw a simple shape of a costume. Make sure the shape you draw is bigger than your hand.

3 Cut out the costume shape. You will now have the front and back of a costume.

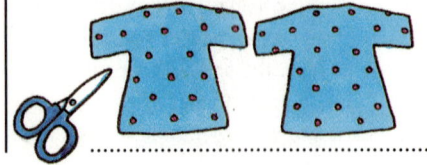

4 Sew, staple or glue the two pieces of cloth together.

5 Decorate the costume. Attach the head to it by stapling or sewing or sticking it firmly.

Operating Glove Puppets

There are different ways of operating glove puppets. Choose the way that you find most comfortable. Practise moving the puppet and speaking for it.

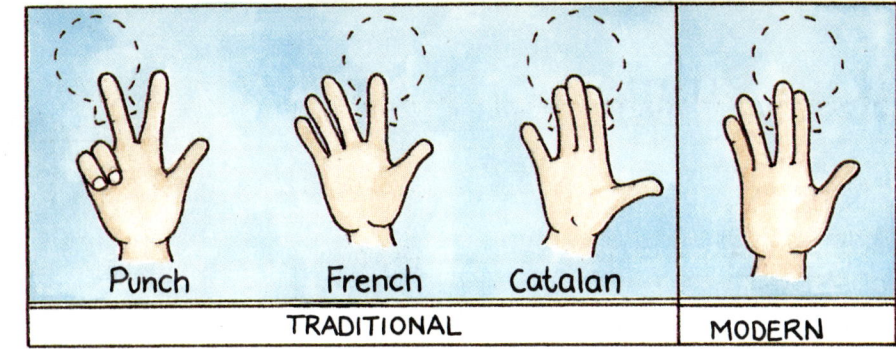

Traditional and modern ways of operating glove puppets

Different Movements of Glove Puppets

1 Try making the puppet wave and clap.

2 Make it look sad by drooping its head and raising one hand as if to wipe away a tear.

3 Hold the puppet's head up and put its hands up to its mouth to make it look surprised.

Rod Puppets

Rod puppets are also known as stick puppets: one main stick makes the body.

A simple rod puppet can be very quick to make and surprisingly effective

Three sophisticated wooden rod puppets

Experiment with the material you use for the puppet's clothes. A stiff cotton will give a very different effect to a light and flowing fabric. Costumes which are loose will disguise the rod and move with the puppet. Very light materials will give a floating and magical appearance. Heavier fabrics will add to the weight of the puppet and operating it may become tiring. Use bold decorative effects and rich colours. Add extra sparkle by adding tinsel, beads and gold or silver paper.

To give the puppet shoulders, use a coat hanger or an empty kitchen roll

String Puppets

String puppets are also known as marionettes. The puppet has moving joints and a string is attached to each leg, arm and to the head.

This marionette has many strings and is capable of very sophisticated movements

The strings are attached to a wooden cross which is tilted to make the puppet move. String puppets are tricky to make and you need a lot of practise before you can move them realistically.

They are operated from above so need a different stage to rod or glove puppets (see page 27).

Sometimes operators of string puppets work without a special theatre. The puppeteers dress in black and stand in the dark behind their puppet.

Simple String Puppets

Take a light, floppy soft toy (a rag doll or teddy bear would work well). Sew or staple strings to each leg and arm. Attach another string to the head. Attach the strings to a coat hanger.

Shadow Puppets

Shadow puppets are held upright on a stick. They are operated from behind a semi-transparent screen. A light, for example, a large torch, is shone from behind the puppet.

The screen is made from thin, lightly-coloured material, tightly stretched and stapled to a wooden frame.

Some of the earliest shadow puppets were made of thin, stretched animal skin, but nowadays they tend to be made of card, lightweight metal or wood.

This is one of the famous shadow puppets from Java. In traditional shadow puppetry men in the audience would watch the puppets while women sat at the other side of the screen and watched the shadows.

A performance of *The Great Mahousi* shadow puppet show

Simple Shadow Puppets

1 Draw a bold outline on a piece of card and cut around it.

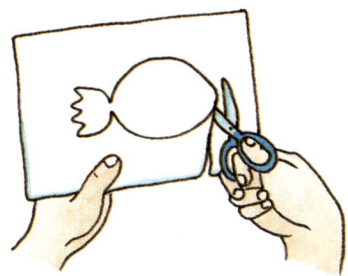

2 Attach a thin stick to the middle of the puppet figure using sticky tape.

sticky tape

3 Add extra detail and colour by piercing holes in the figure and covering the holes with sweet wrappers or coloured cellophane.

use a hole punch to make an eye space

sweet wrappers

17

Recycled Puppets

Puppets can be made from a variety of materials.

Start a collection of interesting scraps:

- Shredded cloth, wool, string, felt and paper make hair.
- Shiny stars, paper, ping pong balls, bottle tops or buttons make eyes.
- Empty kitchen rolls or coat hangers can make shoulders.
- Ribbons, laces, bits of wool and string come in useful for costumes and props.
- Empty boxes and pots can become heads or feet.

Ideas for Recycled Puppets

Try experimenting with different materials to find ideas for puppets. Here are some suggestions.

This rat is made from an old grey sock, a grey jumper, an army gas mask, latex and tissue paper

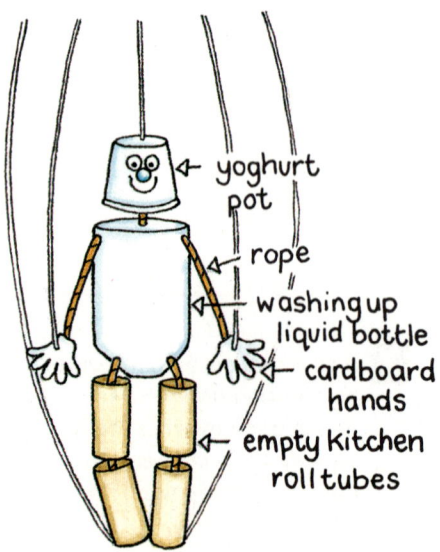

Washing up liquid marionette

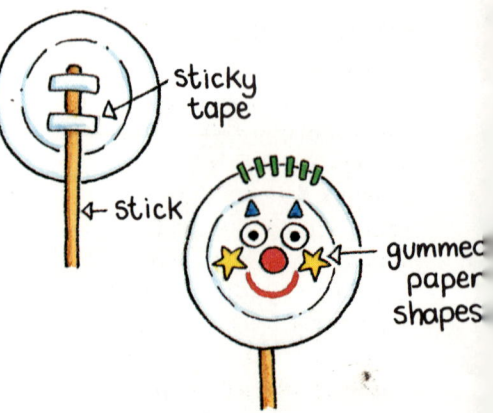

Paper plate rod puppet

Putting on a Performance – The Pied Piper

Schoolchildren put on a puppet show of the Pied Piper. They made the puppets, worked out the script, set up a stage and performed the play.

The Characters

The characters in the Pied Piper story are (from left to right): the rats (recycled puppets); the lame boy who gets left behind (shadow puppet); the Pied Piper (rod puppet with papier mâché head); the Mayor and townsfolk (rod puppets with papier mâché heads); the children (shadow puppets)

The Script

There are many versions of the Pied Piper story. There is a Pied Piper play in the *Pathways* series (Stage 4, Set D) and there are several story versions. There is also the famous poem by Robert Browning. Try reading some of these and decide which is most suitable, or you could write your own version.

If writing your own script, make the puppets first. Then improvise the story. Once the story is roughly worked out, then write it down. Use a highlighter pen to pick out the speeches. Make sure that no one character is speaking for too long. Audiences prefer a performance with plenty of action, movement, sound and effects rather than long speeches.

Performance showing the Pied Piper, the rats and the Mayor

The Pied Piper

In did come the strangest figure.
His queer long coat from heel to head
Was half of yellow and half of red.
And he himself was tall and thin,
With sharp blue eyes, each like a pin.
And light loose hair, yet swarthy skin,
No tuft on cheek nor beard on chin,
But lips where smiles went out and in;
There was no guessing his kith and kin:
And nobody could enough admire
The tall young man and his strange attire.

From *The Pied Piper of Hamelin* by Robert Browning

Read the stories, poems and plays about the Pied Piper to get ideas for his costume and features.

For this Pied Piper a long thin balloon has been used to make the basic head shape. A bent pipe cleaner made the base for a long thin nose. The end of a box has been stuck to the side of the balloon to make ear shape lumps. The ear shapes were covered with papier mâché. Any bulges in the paper mâché were covered over with a thin layer of paper. The head was then left to dry before painting.

Scale

The puppet head can be large or small but if it is being used in a play it should be in scale with the other puppets. In the Pied Piper play, for example, the Piper should be larger than the other characters; he should be much taller and more impressive than the townsfolk. The townsfolk should be larger than the children and the children larger than the rats. Try to keep a sense of scale in mind.

The Pied Piper is a rod puppet – his body is a long stick. The rod is inserted into the head and held in place with strong adhesive tape. His arms have been made from cardboard tubes and are moved by sticks attached to them. His costume is loose and flowing. This will make his movements seem more magical. Sparkling threads and tinsel add to the effect.

The Townsfolk

The Mayor and Townsfolk are all rod puppets with papier mâché heads.

Make props for puppets using a few feathers and ribbons, beads, sweet wrappers, card and even twigs. You could also make brooms, shopping baskets, fishing rods, flags, pipes and hats.

Use your imagination, and any odds and ends you have collected and can recycle.

To individualise a costume, decorate it with buttons, fabric, tinsel etc. Paper doilies would make lace collars and edges for costumes. A bag of chocolate coins can be the money that the Mayor refuses to give to the piper.

The Mayor's chain of office can be made by stringing together some foil-wrapped chocolate coins

The Hamelin Children

Small feet were pattering, wooden shoes clattering,
Little hands clapping and little tongues chattering...
And like fowls in a farmyard when barley
    is scattering,
Out came the children running.
All the little boys and girls,

With rosy cheeks and flaxen curls,
With sparkling eyes and teeth like pearls,
Tripping and skipping, ran merrily after
The wonderful music with shouting
    and laughter.

From *The Pied Piper of Hamelin* by Robert Browning

The line of children can be made as shadow puppets. Fold a piece of card into a zig-zag. Draw the outline of a child on the folded card and then cut the shapes out.

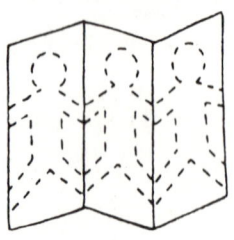

Take a piece of card. Draw a basic shape of a child and cut it out. Some children could be facing forwards, others in profile. Try to add some interest, such as spiky hair, which will look good in outline.

Individualise the children by adding details. Add hair to some, give others props such as hoops, skipping ropes, balloons or other toys. Ribbons and paper lace can also be added. Holes or shapes cut into the shadow puppet add extra detail. Cellophane or sweet wrappers can be used to add colour.

One of the children should stand out as different: the lame boy who gets left behind. He could have a crutch or stick.

The lame boy shadow puppet

The Rats

*Out of the houses the rats came tumbling.
Great rats, small rats, lean rats, brawny rats,
Brown rats, black rats, grey rats, tawny rats.*

From *The Pied Piper of Hamelin* by Robert Browning

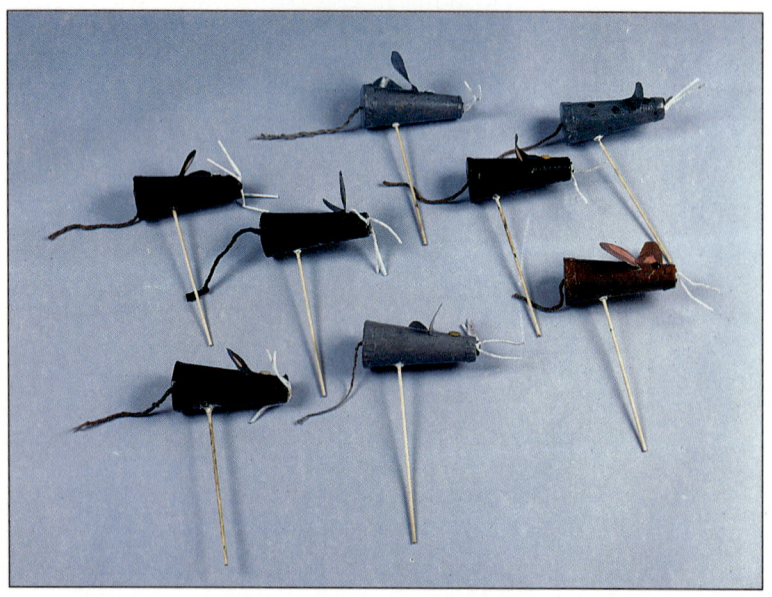

These rats are made from recycled materials

There are many different ways of making a rat puppet. The rats can all be the same, or varied as they are in the poem. Fat or thin rats, big or small rats, rats with snarls or smiles, rats with teeth and rats with moving tails or opening mouths could be made.

To make a simple rat rod puppet, draw and cut out a basic rat shape and attach it to a stick. Add whiskers, fur or felt, and a long plaited string tail to make the puppet more effective.

These rats would also work as shadow puppets (see pages 16-17 for advice on making a shadow puppet).

A glove puppet rat could be made using a grey sock, and adding eyes and whiskers.

The Stage

When the puppets and props have been made, the play can be performed. You will need: a stage, lights, sound effects and plenty of rehearsal.

Pole tied to the side of a chair. A sheet is stretched between the poles and firmly stapled into place.

Screen B is attached to longer poles. Use paper or thin fabric for this screen.

Screen A should be high enough to hide the puppeteers from the audience.

Making a Stage

This stage is suitable for glove and rod puppets. Paint or stick scenery onto Screen B or place a light behind this screen and use it for a shadow puppet performance.

String Puppet Stage

Turn a table over so that it is lying on its side. Stand behind the table to operate the puppet. Wear dark clothes and lean over the puppet so that the attention of the audience is focused on the marionette not on the puppeteer.

Lights and Sound

Lights

If there are lights for the stage, coloured sheets of acetate can be held near the light to change the colour and the atmosphere of a scene.

WARNING! Ensure the acetate is at a safe distance from the light bulb.

Sound Effects

Movement of puppets, atmospheric light and musical accompaniment are sometimes better than words, so do not be afraid to have times in the performance when there are no words spoken.

Recorded music or live music can be played, and try experimenting with sound effects: for example, play a recorder to make the Pied Piper's music. Drums, shakers or other percussion instruments can make the sound of the rats' feet. Start with a gentle pattering of feet then build up to a very heavy pounding. A crash of cymbals would be dramatic as the splash when all the rats jump into the river.

Squeaks can be made by rubbing a wet cork on a bottle. When the mountain closes on the children, make the sound of a closing door, perhaps by slamming a wooden box lid shut. Play or sing parts of songs that fit in with the story. The nursery rhyme 'Girls and Boys Come Out To Play' sung happily and then in a slow, sad tone would work well for the scene where the children follow the Piper and then disappear.

Sounds and music add to the atmosphere

Acting with Puppets

Practise the play. During rehearsals make sure that someone is standing at the back of the room as an audience to check how the effects look and how the puppet movement is working.

Puppeteers must keep as quiet as possible. Any giggling, pushing etc., will be noticed by the audience. Wear dark clothes to help stay out of sight. The puppet's costume should be long enough to hide the puppeteer's arms.

A puppet cannot show a full range of emotion. This has to be conveyed in other ways – by the puppeteer's voice, by lighting, by music and by sound.

Voice

It is hard to be heard clearly when speaking from behind a screen or when operating a puppet, so remember: look up and speak loudly and clearly. Vary the pace of speech. To show a character is excited, speak quickly; if the character is thoughtful or sad, speak slowly. Pause when appropriate. Vary the volume – some words can be spoken, some whispered. Singing and chanting can also be included in the performance.

Operating the Puppets

When performing, hold the puppets high and turn them towards each other if they

are talking to each other. It is important that the audience knows which puppet is supposed to be speaking so puppets who are not speaking in a particular scene should be held still. The speaker should move, turn or wave its arms to draw attention to itself.

Practise moving the puppet to create different moods. For instance, make the shadow puppets of the children skip happily at first. Later they can move slowly as if under a spell.

Many skills are involved in making puppets and putting on a puppet play. By putting on a puppet performance you are taking part in an ancient tradition – a tradition which links different cultures and different ages together. Your own traditions are being created by trying out ideas and inventing new effects.

Index

Page numbers in *italics* refer to photographs or illustrations.

Costumes 12, 14, 22, *22*, 23, 29

Mrs Outside/Inside 6, *6*
Muppets, The *4*

Odessa and the Magic Goat 5

Papier mâché heads 8, *8-9*, 12, *19*, 21, *21*, 23
Props 8, 18, 23, 25
Puppeteers 5, 6, 15, 27, *27*, 29
Puppets:
    acting with 29-30
    features 8, 10-12, *10*, *12*, 21
    movements 7, *7*, *13*, 15
    operating 11, 13, *13*, 15, 16, 29
    simple 7, 11, 14, *14*, 15, 17
Punch and Judy 6, *6*

Sammead, The 4, *4*
Shadow puppet screen 16, *16*, 27

Travelling players 5

31

Further Reading

The Complete Book of Puppetry by David Currell (Pitman)

The Know How Book of Puppets by Philpott and McNeil (Usborne)

Making a Start with Marionettes by Eric Bramall (Bell)

Making Shadow Puppets by Coleman and Bryan (Search Press)

Punch and Judy – a History by George Speaight (Studio Vista)

Puppets by Harriet Blanchard (Wayland)

Puppets by Meryl Doney (Watts)

Puppets and Marionettes by Raymond Humbert (Magnet)

Places to Visit

The Puppet Centre
Battersea Arts Centre
176 Lavender Hill
London
SW11 5TN

Tel: 0171 228 5335

Little Angel Marionette
    Theatre
14 Dagmar Passage
Cross Street
London
N1 2DN

Tel: 0171 226 1787

Cannon Hill Puppet
    Theatre
Midlands Arts Centre MAC
Cannon Hill Park
Birmingham
B12 9QH

Tel: 0121 440 4221

Scottish Mask and Puppet
    Centre
8 Balcarres Avenue
Kelvindale
Glasgow
G12 0QF

Tel: 0141 339 6185